Voices of the City:

Truth, Pain, Healing, Joy and Transformation

I0833710

Copyright © 2026 by City Soul Cafe
All rights reserved. Published in the United States of America.
Second edition.

No part of this book may be reproduced or transmitted in any form, or by any means, electronic or mechanical, including photocopying, recording or by any information storage or retrieval system without written permission from the publisher.

Voices of the City: Truth, Pain, Healing, Joy and Transformation
1st edition
ISBN (Trade pbk.)
979-8-234-07188-0
Layout and Design: Chris Massenburg
Cover Art: JRC3 Graphics & Design

www.citysoulcafe.com

HPJ's Writeeasy Publishing
Durham, North Carolina

City Soul Presents “Voices of the City”

Every city has a heartbeat.

At City Soul Cafe, that heartbeat is poetry.

This anthology captures the voices of poets who have stepped onto the City Soul stage and shared pieces of their truth, pain, healing, joy and transformation.

Inside these pages you will find powerful reflections on identity, love, struggle, resilience, and the life-changing power of poetry.

These are not just poems.
These are testimonies.

From the stage… to the page…
these poets represent the soul of a community that believes words can change lives.

Welcome to City Soul Cafe.

Table of Contents

TIME

Angela Harvey

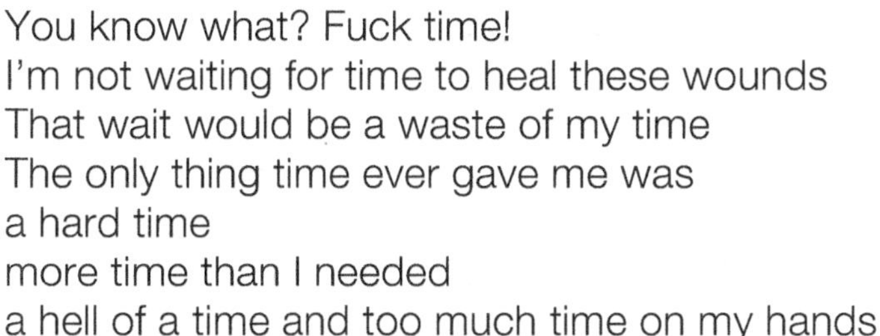

You know what? Fuck time!
I'm not waiting for time to heal these wounds
That wait would be a waste of my time
The only thing time ever gave me was
a hard time
more time than I needed
a hell of a time and too much time on my hands

I mean, what the hell!
Cyndi Lauper's "Time After Time" makes
Prince's "Sign o' the Times"
Seem like a race against time

Time will tell, they say
Well, I think it's about time "they" shut the fuck up
Although it appears I'm having
the time of my life, I'm not!
Hell, daylight even savings time
Always about damn time

Naw, you can miss me with that
It's all in good time
I'll stand the test of time
Three time's a charm
Time doesn't seem to be of the essence
And I don't need time to tell me that

I've been two-timed, and time can kiss my black ass
Time should just fly the fuck out of here
It's only a matter of time
Well, I'm not waiting on time to fix this
Time got me fucked up
Big Time

Lionel Richie did have it right
I am once, twice, three times a lady
And if time were money, I'd be a millionaire
Buying time
Living on borrowed time
With more downtime
Than Florida Evans got good times

I guess I just got bad timing
Or I'm in the right place at the wrong time

Oh snap, look at the time
It seems I've run out of it
I pray my ride to healing is on time and
not kicking it with my hurt, taking its sweet time
It's got to be obvious as hell I'm not making up for lost time

Anyway, thank you all for your time
My ride is finally here, and it's about time!
I'm out of here;
Unless you need me to run that by you one more time

City Soul

Katherine Rose

City Soul is Church
Not your Wednesday night prayer meeting, but the spilling of the scars we've carried since birth
Because shedding our pain, and releasing our shame
May cause someone else to stand up and do the same
The power of transmutation, words into flames
Where mere people, turn to prophets, rise to fame

City Soul is home
From the time you walk in the door you are never alone
Every snap, every cheer, from City Soul is sincere
Giving you courage to overcome your fears
Hugs so tight, they put your soul back together
There's not a storm, together that we can't weather

City Soul is life
For the shedding of our pain, made some of us put down the knife
Drowning our pain in the ink, instead of grabbing the liquor
Because the ink will heal the pain quicker
Or just words placing breath in our lungs
Like our whole lives, had really just begun

City Soul is truth
A family of artist under one roof
Raw emotions, never censored
A place where we can be heard
A place where we can leave it on the stage
Then carry on and keep turning the page

City Soul is the soul of the city
We got that new shit, old shit, and new old shit ready
DJ in the corner, with beats always ready
Champ on the mic, keeping the show running steady

It’s always a party, and we bring the soul
And there's more love in Chubb’s cupcakes, than any bakery holds

Soapbox
Willie Dunmore III

Somebody give me a soapbox

Where the Words Breathe

Leslie "Les" Nash

I don't know much about this life
But I do know one thing

Poetry lives in me

The words sit on my tongue like a secret
Sweet enough to savor
But too heavy not to spill

Rumors turn into run-on sentences
Suspended in the air
Every syllable stretching

Sometimes they arrive in whispers
Barefoot
Tiptoeing across my mind
Like they're afraid to wake the truth

But poetry ain't quiet for long

It stretches my veins
Thumps my chest
Kicks my ribs

Until the quiet feels like suffocation
And words are the only way I breathe

Once a poem finds its breath
It doesn't ask permission
It spills
Over tables
On stages
And to strangers

Poetry ain't something I do
It's something that happens through me

Poetry is where heartache learns to punctuate
It's where pain learns grammar
It's where silence finally loses the argument
It's where the adverse becomes the reverse in verse
It's where heart meets pen
And ink heals

It's where a nobody becomes somebody
It's where a grown baby learns to take its first breath

And the wild thing about poetry
Once it leaves my mouth
It doesn't belong to me anymore

It lands in the ears of strangers
My story starts breathing in someone else's lungs

And suddenly
My truth
Finally
Let's someone else exhale

Poetry saved me from myself

Angie

There were nights my body felt like a crime scene
I didn't report.
Nights where my heartbeat was the only thing in
the room
trying to keep me alive
and even that felt tired.
I remember sitting on the edge of my bed
like it was the edge of a rooftop,
hands trembling,
vision blurry,
my mind whispering things
I'm still ashamed to admit out loud.
I remember the weight
that thick, heavy, suffocating weight
pressing down on my chest
like somebody had climbed inside me
and decided to pull all the light switches off the wall.
I didn't want to die.
I just didn't know how to keep living.
I had nights where I stared at my own reflection and
didn't recognize the eyes looking back.
Eyes swollen from crying,
lips cracked from begging the universe
to give me something
anything
that didn't hurt.
I thought about disappearing.
Not in a poetic way.
Not in some beautiful soft fade to black.
I mean the kind of disappearing
where people would scroll past my last post
and say, "Damn…I didn't know she was struggling."
And that thought alone
almost pushed me further.

Because I was screaming silently
and no one heard it.
But poetry did.
Poetry heard the panic in my breath
and kicked my door open
with no warning,
no softness,
no sugarcoating.
It grabbed me by the wrist
right when I was slipping,
slammed a notebook in front of me,
and said, “If you’re going to bleed,
do it here. I’m not letting you go like this.”
So I wrote.
Ugly.
Messy.
Raw.
Honest.
I wrote the truth I hid from everyone,
the truth I couldn’t even look myself in the eye to say.
I wrote until my tears hit the page
so hard the ink ran.
I wrote until my breathing evened out.
Until my hands stopped shaking.
Until my thoughts stopped sprinting
toward the edge of something final.
Poetry became the room
where I could scream without apology.
Where I could confess the darkest corners
of my mind and not be judged for it.
It let me say, “I wanted to end it,”
But it answered back, “Not tonight. You’re not finished. Your story has more truth than your trauma.”
And slowly…
line by line…
I came back.
I built a bridge out of metaphors
when I couldn’t find the strength

to build one out of hope.
I stitched myself together
with stanzas when my spirit felt too torn to hold anything else.
Poetry didn't save me gently.
It saved me by fighting dirty.
By dragging me out of my own grave
before I lay down in it.
By reminding me that even in my darkest hour,
I was still made of something worth staying for.
And now when I step up to this mic
and speak this truth,
I do it for the version of me
who almost didn't make it.
For the little girl sitting on that bed
with tears in her eyes
and pain in her soul
whose only weapon was a pen.
I do it to honor the woman I became
the one who didn't fold,
didn't vanish,
didn't give the darkness
the ending it wanted.
Poetry didn't just save my life.
It handed it back to me
and said, "Here rewrite yourself. And this time, don't forget how powerful you are.

Poetry is...

CA$H

Poetry is breath
between what happened to you
and what you survived.
It's the space
 between what broke you
 and what built you back
Poetry is truth
 with the volume turned all the way up.
Not polished.
 Not pretty.
Just honest
enough to make a room full of strangers
 feel seen.
It's the moment a trembling hand
stops shaking
because the pen finally said
what the mouth was afraid to.

Poetry is memory breaking out of silence
Because it refuses to stay buried.
Poetry is where I come from.
Brooklyn sidewalks,
 where stories bounce off brownstones
 and the train tracks keep rhythm
 for every dream trying to get out.
I learned early—
 in places I call home,
 if nobody gives you a mic
 you build one out of courage.
Because poetry is survival.
It's turning scars
into syllables.
Grief into rhythm.
Life into language.

and Pressure into power.

Turning silence
 into something that refuses
 to stay quiet.

Poetry is the pen
 becoming a shovel
 digging truth
 out of my chest.

Some people write poems.
While others live them.

Poetry is rhythm.
Heartbeat.
 Footsteps on pavement.
 The late-night hum of a city
 that never stopped teaching me
 how to speak.
A good poem doesn't just whisper in your ear—
 it reminds the world that it has a soul.

Poetry is confession
 without a courtroom.
It's the soul standing naked
 without shame.
Poetry is when the quiet ones
 become thunder.
When stories buried in rib cages
 kick the door open
 and demand air.

Pain is heavy—
 poetry is how we carry it.

Poetry is a bridge.
Between strangers.

Between silence and sound.
Between who you were
and who you're becoming.

Poetry is a mirror.
Sometimes it shows you beauty.
Sometimes it shows you bruises.
But every time—
it shows you truth.
Poetry can save you or expose you.
But every time—
it tells the truth.

And the truth about poetry is this:
It doesn't ask permission
to exist.

It shows up
in the chest,
in the throat,
in those shaking hands
that finally decide to speak.

Every poem ever written
is a voice refusing
to disappear.
Every poem ever written
is a soul
leaving fingerprints on time.

Because every poem ever written
is really just a human being saying—
I survived this moment.

Poetry is proof
that the human spirit
refuses to stay quiet.
And if my voice echoes long after I'm gone,

then poetry wasn't just something I wrote…
It was proof
that I was here.

Lost Girl

Rune, The Artist

When I found poetry

I was 17 and heartbroken

Once again my chest had been emptied by a prince in sterling silver

And I found myself empty, like a wet glass on a hot day

Lifeless

Worthless

Doom scrolling through YouTube, I landed on a video of a man

Edwin

He told me what happens when a boy says 'I Love You' and never before then did I believe

That a feeling could be put into words that can paint pictures

Words that can change my perception; rewrite my paradigm

When I found poetry, I found my voice

That my story was meant to go beyond a notebook discussion

And as I wrote, I could hear music, percussion

Melodies becoming remedies to my previous reckoning

I began writing ballads that kept my heart beating

I learned that a craft doesn't start with perfection, just an emotion

That my worth wasn't limited to my own perception, and rather it needed redirection

The lines I once wrote on my arms told no testimony to how far I had come

So I started writing more, so a new story could be told

When I found poetry, I found my spark

My bedroom floor played home to Composition notebooks and pens

But never would I reopen them to read again,

To feel again

Never did I let myself believe that someone else needed to see

Everything I hid from me

So I continued to search; digging for gold behind videos of hurt, pain, and truths

Digging for memories in scrap papers,

And finally cleaning my room

When I found poetry, I found myself

I found the little girl I still was, who was told to keep quiet

Banging against my ribcage in protest

Begging to be heard

Praying to be seen

Saying to me 'I'm ready!' behind my chest

So, when I found poetry, she really found me,

Waiting.

From The Inside Out

Sherrita C W Delacruz

Instead, he became a penitentiary bound pupil of an institutionalized life and mentality

Brilliant but dumb at the same time

Leaving children fatherless

Going in
Coming out
Going in
Coming out for years

And years and years yet

Audacious enough to blame anyone but himself for his children being the way they were

Reared without a father
Wonder why the mothers couldn't stand him for that.
Male presence is pivotal in raising children
Mamas cannot do it all
But bear the great responsibility in trying to be everything a child needs
Pride comes before the fall

Especially in the case of young mommies
looking for love in the wrong places

Thug passion spilled on a rose that grew from concrete
A beautiful nightmare
An appetite for destruction conceived
Prepped with convincing yet false statements
Motions of discovery without giving anyone up

Because this life two created
Ain't going no where

Neither are the excuses for the paternal absence

Many years past attempted to fulfill the dream
deferred upon release

But went back as quickly as a crack sale
A heroin hit or even a minor misdemeanor
Violating time wasted

What's worse than the lack of financial help to care for another life for many long years?

The inability to console abandonment issues tainting the confidence of a growing mind?

The trial and error placement of step daddies and
blended family broken?

Proof beyond a reasonable doubt huh?
Nobody ever screamed free Lorenzo except baby girl
Not even him

The reality was too much

Way easier to stay inside and gamble Debbie cakes cigarettes and contraband I guess

Paytel calls on another nigga name cause nobody on the outside care enough no more

To even wanna take 10 minutes of they life to hear the lies

Let alone put another dime on them books

Aunt no such thing as halfway crooks

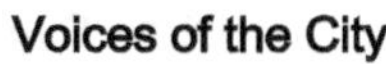

They all in
up to and including

Breaking the code of fatherhood

That’s deeper than any felony

The Great Chillien

Esoteric Lyrist

The Great Chillien
I was nine…
when the world bent sideways on my spine,
when innocence cracked like chalk outlines
and silence tried to copyright my lifeline.
Nine…
when shadows tiptoed into my childhood,
when fear learned my name
and used it like a passcode
to places it should've never stood.
But trauma didn't trademark me—
it just tried.
And every time it whispered, "you're mine,"
I replied,
"Watch me redefine—
'cause what you tried to claim, God already signed…
in ink that doesn't fade and a signature divine."
Back then, quiet was my camouflage—
I stitched hush into my breathing,
made my ribs a secret garden
where my tears could grow without leaving.
But even gardens have seasons,
and one day my roots refused the weeping—
turns out God got a green thumb…
even pain has to follow what He's planting and keeping.
I grew teeth.
I grew truth.
I grew thunder in my speaking—
like Heaven tapped my vocal cords
and said, "yeah… we're gonna need that for a reason."
'Cause nine wasn't my downfall—
it was just my training season.
Life came swinging in sequels,
trying to remake the same trauma

with new cast members and new reasons.
Friendships ghosted.
Loves folded.
Family storms hit without warning—
but I weathered every forecast,
'cause grace stayed covering me
like it knew I'd be important in the morning.
Built different—
not by accident, but intention,
like God wrote light in my story
and told darkness, "you don't get final mention."
Plot twist:
what broke others built me better—
guess pressure and purpose
been in partnership forever.
And then—
My father.
My solid ground.
My trusted sound.
Cancer crept in
stealing days like a thief who knew his way around.
I watched the strongest man I knew
fight a war in his own cells—own cells
while I held on to every moment
like it was the last bead
on a fragile string of farewell… fair well.
When he passed—
my universe cracked open,
and grief tried to take the wheel,
but Daddy didn't raise me
to stall on an uphill.
I heard him whisper,
"Stand tall, baby…
your strength is still real."
And underneath that whisper—
something deeper, calmer… steel—
like God said, "I got you,"
in a language only broken hearts can feel.

Lowkey…
God is funny like that—
won't stop the storm every time,
but will make sure you don't drown in the aftermath.
So I rose—
with heartbreak in my pocket,
and resilience in my stride.
With the echo of his courage
and a Spirit I couldn't deny.
But hear me:
my story ain't a museum of pain
with tragedies displayed in frames.
My story is an engine—
and every scar became octane.
Every setback?
Just propane.
Every heartbreak?
Main vein.
Fuel for the fire—
but God controlled the flame,
so what was meant to consume me
just refined me—
had me coming out cleaner
with the same fire, different name.
I'm not a victim—
I'm the victory.
The living, breathing remix of history.
The alchemy where broken pieces
turn into brilliancy—
divinely designed chemistry.
The synergy
of legacy and energy
and a little bit of heaven in me
rising endlessly—
like God said, "watch this,"
and made a testimony outta what was testing me.
I rise—
like Harriet hid a map in my bones,

like Angela tucked courage in my tones,
like every ancestor invested stock
in my milestones—
and God stamped approval
before I ever claimed what was my own.
I rise—
not as the sum of what hurt me,
but as the proof that pain
could never convert me.
Couldn't divert me.
Couldn't desert me—
'cause even in valleys,
God doesn't do abandonment; He just does surgery.
Yeah—
cut deep, heal deeper,
closed wounds speaking like preachers.
I turned every wound into a workspace
and healed myself so thoroughly
it felt like Heaven had rehearsed me—
like grace kept calling my name
until I answered it personally.
I'm not the wound, I'm the warrior,
not the fall, I'm the floor-raiser,
not the pain, I'm the page-changer,
rewriting fate with a flame that refuses danger.
I'm the thunder they can't quiet,
the riot that won't retire,
the spark that became a wildfire—
but even fire knows boundaries
when God the one who inspired.
Pressure built empires,
but purpose took it higher—
'cause when God breathes on it,
even ashes aspire.
Call me comeback in high definition—
the revision, the risen edition,
the walking definition
of "nothing you did could cancel my mission"—

'cause what God authored in me
doesn't come with human permission.
I don't just rise—
I soar past the ceiling you set.
I don't just heal—
I collect every scar like a debt.
I don't just live—
I live loud, and without regret.
Nine didn't break me,
Life didn't take me,
and every breath I speak now
is the victory God gave me—
and if you hear me…
if you laughing just a little
while you still fighting heavy…
that's Him too—
God has range…
can turn pain into purpose
and still sneak joy in steady.
So if you breathing through a battle
you never asked to face—
just know:
the same God who kept me steady
is keeping you in place.
Same grace.
Same hand.
and if He brought you this far?
He's not the type to cancel plans.

Definition: Black Girl

By Neeka

Being a black girl means more to me than skin tone
It's more than melanin, more than curves carved in stone
More than thick lips, soft hips, culture in our bones
More than rhythms in our walk, more than songs in our tone

Being a black girl means more than the weight on our shoulders
More than stories they told us, more than what history folders
Tried to box us in with chains and cold nights growing colder
We are fire, we are gold, we are brilliance getting bolder

More than the past they tried to bury in pain
More than the lashes, the loss, and the chains
We are the daughters of queens who broke every chain
And planted new gardens where sorrow once reigned

Give us our flowers
WE are that six percent with degrees
WE are the pedigree
We are the WE
We are the ME
We are the YOU
We are the TRUTH
THE WAY and the light

Created in His image and not out of spite
Not just alright
We're top tier
We are the feared

We're not the anger they portray us to be
We're the ones cultivating the boardroom dreams
With glowing brown skin that shines like the sun
And minds sharp as blades,
our victories won

We are the brilliance in midnight hues
Intelligence wrapped in cocoa and blues
Skin kissed by galaxies, radiant and wise
With knowledge and power behind our eyes

We are the descendants of Harriet Tubman's courage in flight
Who led whole nations to freedom at night
Of Madam C. J. Walker's empire and might
The first self-made millionaire, shining so bright

Of Maya Angelou's pen that soared
Her words like wings, her voice adored
Of Shirley Chisholm who dared to stand
The first Black woman to run for the land

Of Katherine Johnson's numbers in space
Guiding rockets with brilliance and grace
Of Michelle Obama's poise and pride
A First Lady who walked with the world at her side

We are scientists, poets, mothers, and queens
Doctors and lawyers, creators of dreams
Our skin is a story the sun chose to write
Our brilliance a beacon, our future is bright

We are our ancestors' whispered prayers
Their wildest dreams walking up stairs
Their hymns, their hope, their sacred cries
Now living and breathing in our brown eyes

So NO we are not just pain and despair
We are silk in the sunlight, crowns in the air
Our history is kingdoms, scholars, and art
Not chains on our wrists, but crowns on our heart

We are rhythm and reason, beauty and brains
We are sunshine after ancestral rains

No longer just stories of sorrow and strife
Being a Black girl to ME means living in light.

Far From Home - (What Poetry Is To Me)

By Quan

They say distance makes the heart grow fonder
I'm starting to believe that
The longer I've been away from poetry
this stage
I realize
I need that
The only place that separates reality from what they perpetuate
I guess you can call it my safe space
Safe from perspectives that only
Interjects
when it's to their benefit

Safe from those demons that don't quite fit in the box we put them in
So we make them bend to fit

Safe from the PTSD that comes
when you write these lines

Safe from toxic comparisons telling you
what's been refurbished

Can't be refined

Healing sometimes sounds like…
I went out today
I prayed this morning
I ate today
I didn't automatically denounce it when someone told me
It's gone be okay

Grace

is how I've survived and standing on the fact

I don't like to feel this way
My reflection and I are in a mirror match
Separated from bad habits
that still appear attached

Trying to tell my temptations
relax

This is get back
Get back
to the man I know I am

Get back
To writing these lines
and being clear on where I stand

Get back
to that locked in mindset
That got me in this bag

I'm confident enough to say I've made it through
But humble enough not to brag

I keep God close even when I'm not in alignment
Understanding that these contracts
with new contacts
Always come with fine print
Didn't know the consequences that came with going
from
Mediocre to fine shit
Letting the results of the gym and being told

I'm him

Put the goal of it all
in confinement

I'm confused on the dating scene

And how it relates to me
Don't know if it's latency
or if God
has someone he's making wait for me
Patiently

Knowing I'll soon find that path that he made for me

Of it's too late

I mean

Maybe he's tired of me making the same mistakes
He gives me time to be on time
but somehow
I still show up late
Reminders of past relations don't seem to go away
Quick to stay back from connection not knowing
When people will go astray
Thinking this is "it"
with every connection
Just for it to float away
Same universal advice when it comes to finding it

Yea I know

"one day"

But one thing that doesn't move

Is always there even when
I'm not in the mood
The only thing that speaks from
The soul of me

It's poetry…

Annotate

Aavillure

Dear poetry,
you taught me my first words through the boombox

You started in the dark then,
evolved in the Bronx,
Into boom bap,
James brown vinyl's spinning in the park

But for me it was a CD entry in the top with a Lloyd banks tape in

It was if I never heard words before a day in my life
you put these words in a seven year old as I plopped down in front of your sound just to jot to get it

words that are rhythmic
made time a gimmick
And these words they transcend me,
transplant me
into whoever these syllables decide
And that choice of who I wanted to be wasn't always mine

every thought became
Annotated
with Luda, big and em records
Wayne and pain
and Kim records 500 degrees and Carter one through three

You know?
them records

Aquemini and life after death

You know,
them records

And crime mob taught me to knuck if you buck
And Kendrick brought us the big steppers

Your vibe, taught me how to vocalize long after I uttered a vowel

like I found my vocal cords on the groove of Andre three thou'
Missy with Timbaland sound and Ceelo with I'll be around

Contributing to every line I've ever pen down

But —

that was before the takeover the waits over nigga
then I learned the god MC Rakim before Hova
Slick Rick had me wanting the chains, the gold rope ones
then meth had me hitting replay before his verse done
Mary saying no will do blending right into the melodies of Sade
Adu

Mariah, Luther, the Johnson brothers El Debarge and the crew

My love of the fabric of storytelling developed

Then my strawberry letters ensued
With the inspirations of my love from within
Singing

It wasn't me, slim shady told me to do it again!
Like damn, how much undoing of damage you can do with a
pen?

These writtens gave me a sanctuary to be truthful and mend

Life is my ghostwriter,

And my wrist winds through a stencil of everything that I been throughannotated and conflated with these consummate symbols

Of logos on chest cause growth and beauty was never to be gentle

So my soul continues—

To chase—

The CD players in the headrest In a cars leather wrapped to everything but the display

Ushering my confessions to these leaflet presses
Til every page behind it a carbon copy to 30 years of all my lessons

Poetry be my leverage

Pushing and pulling me in and out of this world

So I speak til I feel like Jay Z in that 4.6

And breathe in disappointment and exhale choices

And the answer of what would I do without the sound
That found me before I discovered myself

and went soul searching for who I am together.

Poetry Saved My Life

Jordan Ashley

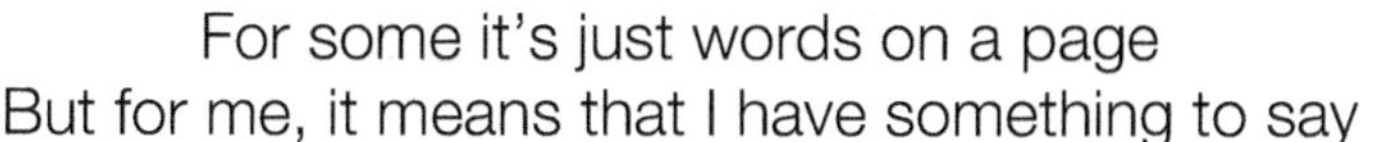

For some it's just words on a page
But for me, it means that I have something to say

Some superheroes wear capes while some are the ones that decides our fate

The words on the page became my saving grace
A superhero without a face

Poetry saved my life

Something that started out as just a hobby growing up, not knowing how impactful it would be

Just like how a pen needs a person in order to write, is how I need the words in order to fight.

Poetry saved my life

Pageant crowns that outweigh you
Thoughts that consume you
Grief that takes over you
Health issues that confuse you

Left with my conversations with God and my pen
The only two things that keeps me Zen
Because for me…it's never been just a trend

Poetry saved my life
In more ways than I can count

The gift from God that keeps on giving
It's amazing how many ways God disguises himself to keep us living

Lost to Fame

Lady T

Crime is on the rise turning all the blue skies to Grey.
Yesterday a kid bled under one.
No one to save him for the fame that came,
gave him too much clout
and when them boys found out they wanted their cut.
Ten rounds to the car
them boys blue just too far couldn't get there in time to save him.
The lies the media will tell cause
that boy tried and failed to leave the hood behind him.
Too smart, true to his heart
he gave love and received it back tremendously.
Fans pour out showing without a doubt
that even after death you still getting clout, so who really won here.
Dead over a lil bread
you made lil brother bled
and got all his affiliates too.
Put on the other shoe
would you want this done to you
cause the way you going it's just a matter of time.
How I wish to hear that last rhyme
but looks like he out time
and I will just have to find comfort in his memories.

Soul Lapse
Destiny Kincaid

I can see it falling apart
At the heart
The little bit of joy that's left
Is in the breath of the dying and the dead

Youth's emotions broken down and eroded like acidic corrosion

Compassion disregarded
Replaced by self-preservation
No simple happiness
No impish elation
{and} No, absolutely No

Hesitation at destruction and desecration

Lack of patience
Perchance
Perhaps a soul lapse
Apocalypse?
Is that what it is

A slow meandering of conscience
Is creation creating the ultimate breakdown

Due to the fact that the "Garden of Eden" lays not within their chest

{but} has been laid to rest by evolutionary genetics

Not by fire
Not by flood

Not by any sickness carried in the blood

Not by earthquake
Or any disaster of any known kind
Just a small twist in the complex mind of mankind

Who is guardian of weapons
Who's at the hilt of every gun?
Hear the flutter of their heartbeat at the term...
"6 million ways to die, choose one"

{or} "my weapon is for killing but my gun is just for fun"

When you see it, you think thugs
When you hear it, you think drugs

{but} There are militant millions claiming values too wholesome

Whole - - - Sum
Mathematically complex
There are more of us than them
But, they could wipe us out by tens

Hole - - - some
Missing that individual spark
All dressed the same with no last name
Always stomping around in a march
"hark who goes there"
Resting among the ranks
young bodies tear inside out

They cry as they attempt to violate their open minds

And lock them down
Rip the Gortex from their chests
While at their muscular best
A mental waste
The pen stops
No carried note is heard
No elaborate colors or shapes

Not one single artistic word
Around the globe an evil is succeeding

Take this as a warning
Look… look… look…
And see

That it doesn't happen to you
Me – he – she
Or our own babies
Peace

When I found myself I…

Poetry Tag

When I found myself I…
Found the true essences of learning to love from outside in. *~Church Da'Poet*

When I found myself I…
I squeezed myself out of the suffocating hold of the cramped cocoon, and grabbed hold of that breath of clean rich air I had been gasping for over the years in this tank of mustard gas I call the world.
My dream went from being a Raisin in the Sun to a succulent grape that soaked my dry lips and filled my aching stomach. *~Maestra Emcees*

When I found myself I…
I went
Down the path parallel to the high road.
Where the wild flowers were sown.
Stitched into the textile
landscapes of memories.
Verbiage of lost tongues,
twisted in poems and psalms.
Rubbed together bearing the friction of nonfiction truths
sung in vibrant vibratos.
Vast expanse in the lyrical sense.
Penny for the thoughtful.
Full of loss for the one soul.
~James King

When I found myself I…
She was sitting on the dock,
dangling her feet in the lake
Giggling
I've been waiting for you…
~Tyamica Mabry

When I found myself I...
I found myself camouflaged in the world around me
Slowly I stood up, shedding societal expectations
I let my colors shine and began to dance
~Mandie Roberston

When I found myself I...
I found love,
the kind of love that's unconditional.
Love so strong you can feel it in your bones.
So I walk different,
talk different
& see the world different.
~CaSandra Lindsey ♡Queen Chosen♡

When I found myself I...
I was just waking up from a cold sweat
turns out it was just last night's squirt spot still wet!
I rolled over and still felt chills up my spine finding myself in his eyes in his eyes in his charm so divine. However lonely I must be.... It truly was a wet dream!
~Parson Nicole Michelle

~

When I found myself I...
I... I did that thing...
you know,
the thing that was forbidden,
that only the forbidden know but the truth seeks...
~Monica Wilcher

When I found myself I...
I found that I wasn't who they wanted me to be.
I was just me,
she,
her...
and I'm okay with that.
~Amy Williams

When I found myself I...
I found true happiness
I found the peace in sitting alone
I found the strength and power of my thoughts
I found ME
~Lee Milla

When I found myself I...
I found my voice to speak out loud and it was freedom.
Freedom like no other,
freedom to choose my independence
~Shaquina Holmes

When I found myself I...
I found myself emerging into something completely new,
naked and free,
for once noticing parts of me I've never known...
this was always the plan
~Angel Triplett

When I found myself I...
I realized the world didn't move an inch,
but I finally woke up and saw the cracks in the old floorboards.
I tried to shrink back into the person I was,
but that version of me is dead and gone.
It's a spit in the face to my growth to pretend I still fit in those narrow spaces.
I am different now,
and I'm not asking for permission to be powerful.
~Malinda Song Alford

When I found myself I...
Learned that the person I see in the mirror is my priority.
I found a universe of possibility.
Let the world fall away.
~Mittie Zellner Lees

When I found myself I…
listened to my voice,
My limbs stretched wide, carrying all I had become,
And there, I blossomed into something new.
~Silnettra Barnhill

When I found myself I…
I found a pile of imperfect pieces,
begging to be made and remade,
shaped a bit more like myself each time.
~Joseph Reese Anderson

When I found myself I…
I found reflections in the undertow that refused to drown me
~Jeff "Unorthodocks" Gary

When I found myself…
Because only then could I see my whole heart and all the other parts working together...
~Jasme Kelly

When I found myself I…
I found more than me.
I found faith, hope, and peace.
Whatever comes I can face it.
because I found more than myself.
~Destiny Kincaid

When I found myself I…
I found someone who was buried alive
and these true essences helped me discover a will to survive.
A purpose to love again,
and not just someone else but me.
~Yochana Israel

When I found myself I…
Found freedom
A freedom to live how I please
An escape from the bounds of society
~Katherine Rose

When I found myself I…
I found a way to rise from my brokenness
~Michelle Chantre'

When I found myself I…
Found a space that allowed my hurt to cry. I found myself more eager to live than die wading in the shallowest of moments asking for forgiveness for being me. I found patients that gave me the 3 g's. God, Giada and Grace.
~Church Da'Poet

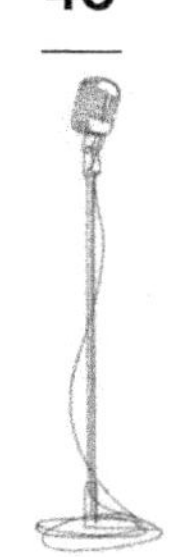

YOUR VOICE

Church Da'Poet

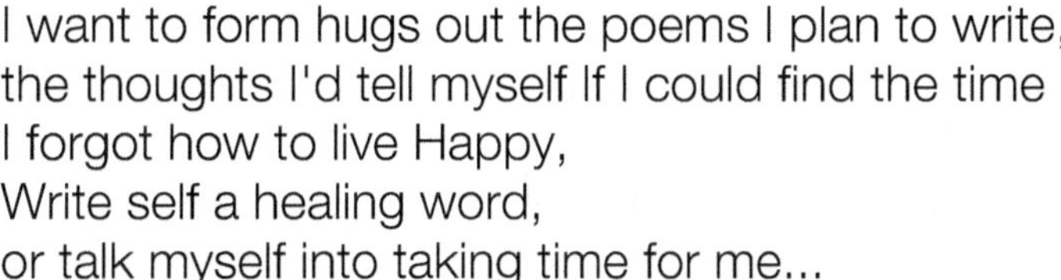

I want to form hugs out the poems I plan to write,
the thoughts I'd tell myself If I could find the time
I forgot how to live Happy,
Write self a healing word,
or talk myself into taking time for me...

In retrospect,
my gift is poison
and the only person with a cure,
hides behind excuses...
the starts
but don't finish times,
brilliant ideals
great smarts
but lacks follow through,
so my poems are missing the points,
I'm handing out assist,
cause my arms can't seem to reach
touch the sky with the fingertip ballpoint,
tired of smudging or balling
up the plans,
I'm a scratched project,
Multi-silver artist,
with the passion to create the world with 6 blinks
My father created it in 6 days...
I weigh the outcome in books and cd's
souls saved and lives touched,
beacon the latitude,
forced my smile to bleed longitude...

I want to script the perfect scenario of how my life should have went,
but of course,
I can't find the time

escape, escape...
Reflection tells Shadow
I am broken glasses of reflected origin of mirrors and shadows,
trees and shade...
doors closed but heart left open.
coral reef of deserted oasis.
a pond full of lake water and doubt.
A spring full of distractions...
leaked into.
streamed feelings,
We LIVE now...
cause there once lived a poet
who never saw a stage in his life he couldn't conquer...
Watched others destroy the passion inside,
till I hid inside my own world.
Ready or not
I busted in the walls of my depression,
and filled the walls with eyes,
I was determined to resurface a new...
but a new meant I had to leave the old me...
he was southern comfort and lemonade,
he was cool and refreshing,
tart, and hard to take without warning.
he was verbally abusive to microphones...
he was a poem beater,
and convicted of domestic pen abuse...
I drained her of all her worth...
Sentence to Live in between the breaths and the pages.
I was booked...
now being sold to the highest bidder.
I for bid-her to leave me again...
recovering POEM-aholic
there is a revival sitting at the edge of my tongue,
dangling,
waiting,
for the first gust of wind to
through caution to the breeze

and jump
no parachute,
just ear waxed
canals,
of jubilee busting between your mucus membrane,
an ordain ministry
of healing and convictions
swinging from the molecules
like Spiderman spawn webs
I am hanging on for
dear life
you haven't always been pleasant,
so I wanted to write excuses
for how you treated one of God servants,
the organ
God gave me to use is waiting for the embrace
signed

YOUR VOICE

Glass Case

Dasan Ahanu

We be the children of glass blowers.
Pious crafters who work
with hands clasped together and
knees touching the earth.
Earth that taught them how
to bear fruit, birth things that grow,
and give to others
until they die.
Glass blowers whose wishes
to the carpenter
that sits on high
become part and parcel promises,
components of glass cases
covering us in grace.

We pieces of wonder...
We be knick knack,
trophy, and
admirable qualities well sewn together
and draped on mannequins.
We be fine china,
snapshots of happy and unsure, and
memories of times past
longing for tomorrow to come.
We be the things none have had
or that others have had but
no longer want.

We sit on thrones
that become tombs and
on stages that
become prisons.
The plate at the bottom
holds the names we are given

but may or may not have earned.
It sits there until replaced
by numbers, a dash, and
remembrances rewritten
by guilt and could have been's.

The spots you notice on the outside
are not bruises.
They are the smudges
I pray the next caretaker
will Windex clean.
What's in here is priceless
but closed off.
Too many have fiddled
with the lock hoping to
pry openness and
expose what's inside.
Some have even tried the smash
and grab hoping to bully
their way in.
Thank God our mothers have
unwavering faith.
They have prayed and cried
until the vision of us is
shatterproof, bulletproof,
though still not protected
from the trauma of seeing
the attempts come and go.
Why won't they learn that
they key is in our eyes?

When your purpose and destiny,
worth and wisdom,
aptitude and ability
are on display
you learn what a fetishizing gaze
feels like.

You learn that gawking
is a seductive
dance with voyeurs whose
admiration is a selfish satisfaction.
That sometimes presence
isn't possibility,
it's just momentary possession.
Without the key though
it's just a traveling exhibition.

You and me,
we know these glass cases
oh too well.
These cursed gifts
of safe distance and deniability.
We know too many living rooms
we never considered home,
too many bedrooms
we never felt completely comfortable in.
We have felt trapped in hallways
where people seem too eager
to pass our pain by.
Know too well that shrines
can be adored or despised
but still left to dust or decay.

We be held on to
for others to enjoy.
We be look but don't touch.
We be window shopping fantasy.
That one day I'll be able
to get that.
That I don't know if that's for me.
We be looked at.
Look at that.
Come here and look at this.
Look now.
Look later.

Walk past with nose up
and never look at all.
Arrogant assurance telling yourself
that it'll be there
when I want to look again.

We
the children of glass blowers.
We be here.
Help up by divinity,
shielded by hope
in glass cases
for all the world
to see

www.ingramcontent.com/pod-product-compliance
Lightning Source LLC
LaVergne TN
LVHW010545100826
845148LV00013B/2618
* 9 7 9 8 2 3 4 0 7 1 8 8 0 *